DISAPPARITIONS

DISAPPARITIONS

JOSEPH HARRINGTON

BLAZEVOX[BOOKS]
Buffalo, New York

publisher ofweird little books

BlazeVOX [books]

blazevox.org

21 20 19 18 17 16 15 14 13 12 01 02 03 04 05 06 07 08 09 10 11

BlazeVOX

Acknowledgements

Portions of "Spies in the Living House" appeared previously in *BlazeVOX, Colorado Review, Mudlark*, and *Spacecraftproject*.

"Dear Future," originally appeared in *Court Green*.

"The Eyes" originally appeared in *Allium*.

The author thanks these publications and their editors.

Many thanks, too, to those who read and offered generous comments on the manuscript in its various stages: C.S. Giscombe, Tony Trigilio, Siobhán Scarry, Giselle Anatol, Susan Schultz, Judy Roitman, and MariaAna Garza. Any flaws are solely the doing of the author.

. . . the one whose writing/not writing only came together as she came together with the object, with the reality of fictions and the unrealities of the facts; the slightly mad one who kept saying, 'There's something in the room with us' . . .

— Avery Gordon, *Ghostly Matters: Haunting and the Sociological Imagination*

Contents

DISAPPARITIONS

To Be Alive Is to Be Haunted

by the prospect of being alive, the fear of wasting your life fearing you're wasting your life. I am me because my little dog haunts me. My senses, too, always handing me images to handle. To be hunted by the light of the moon who finds you out, who sees two monster rabbits generate spontaneously from the garden of bones. Take off your shoes, cover your mouth, leave the roots in the ground. But still the circulating sun will chase you from the other side. Darling poets, franchise a parallel thirst. *Now I can make you whatever I want*, predator, pretty, tall grass, me tall in mountain, me impersonating corpse. Something watches your shoulder. Something will get you yet.

Spook

1. A spectre, apparition, ghost. Often somewhat *jocular* or *colloquial*.
[First in American usage 1801]

2. *slang* (originally and chiefly *U.S.*). An undercover agent; a spy.
[First in American usage 1942; last example 1979]

3. *slang* (originally and chiefly *U.S.*). A derogatory term for a black person.
[First in American usage 1945; last example 1977]

- from *Oxford English Dictionary*

*

Soon afterwards, when I mentioned the mysterious radio at breakfast, Austerlitz told me he had always imagined that the voices moving through the air after the onset of darkness, only a few of which we could catch, had a life of their own, like bats, and shunned the light of day. In the long, sleepless nights of recent years, he said, when I was listening to the women announcers in Budapest, Helsinki, or La Coruña, I often saw them weaving their erratic way far out in the air, and wished I were already in their company.

— W.G. Sebald

My dad's Hammerlund HQ 100-A shortwave radio—bigger than a breadbox (and we *had* a breadbox)—outsized Bakelite knobs, illuminated dials. Good for a spaceship control panel. The vacuum tubes shot dots of light through the riddled steel case onto the walls. My dad taught me to tune with a fine touch: the slightest of movements could bring you out of the barking static and electronic glissandos, into the clearing where somebody spoke.

I went after the cards and pennants the stations would send you for a credible reception report—the wall was covered with them, from the four corners of the earth. The most coveted ones meant finding the faintest signals—like listening for the rare bird in a forest of cackling crows. But the most interesting sounds I heard were on frequencies between the official government-run stations, where chaos ruled— auditory detritus—partial sentences, pulsing bursts of noise, Theremin-sounding waves or blasts of distorted brass bands, dopplering into the dark. Someone speaking, muffled, as through a cloth.

And someone saying lists of random numbers. And repeated foreign words. Or a phrase of music-box music, played over and over and over. Some of these could be accounted for—say, an "interval signal" to mark a station's frequency when it was not broadcasting a program (usually the first measure of a national anthem). But some could not. They were Unidentified Frequency Objects. They could have been Martians; they could have been spirits; and really, what's the difference. Existences from some other side, trying to send a message; spirits respirating forth to earthly receivers, repeating their phrases and numerals, again and again.

Freud associates repetition-compulsion with the death drive, so perhaps the dead are driven to repeat the most quotidian of utterances for eternity.

Years later, a British government official would say, "These are what you suppose they are."

*

Spook from Dutch *spook*   orig *spoek*   the little spook is *spoekje*   the many spooks are *spoken*   *Bent u spokken?*   *Spoken bestaan niet!*   or some such   *Fûgelspoek* = bird ghost   (scarecrow)   Or: *nachtspoek*, which sounds pretty bad   *Seespoek* trans "sea monster," but really scarier IMO   Then   *âldspoek*   — "ugly evil old woman" (always scariest of all,   somehow,   to the spooksayers

*

Almost as soon as radio existed, people began hearing the voices of the dead on the air. Bereaved families listened for words wedged in edgewise on the unused frequencies—the dear departed squeezing in the shortest of messages, or even cries— phrases discerned through the aural fog of interference. Indeed, Marcel O'Gorman claims that "most of the early footage recorded" on gramophone and film "was an attempt to capture death, ghosts, and doppelgangers."

Those technologies became available during the heyday of Spiritualism. Society for Psychical Research co-founder William James "had compared the brains of sitters at séances to Marconi stations," writes John Durham Peters; and "Rudyard Kipling had compared very early radio communications to a séance." In 1877, *Scientific American* wrote of the phonograph, "Speech has become, as it were, immortal." And, as Peters points out, "That 'as it were' is the dwelling place of the ghosts." And why not? "Indeed, all mediated communication is in a sense communication with the dead, insofar as media can store 'phantasms of the living' for playback after bodily death." Or before.

But the first radio messages delivered by spooks disappoint. In the first "controlled experiment" to attempt to record their voices as transmitted through a radio (mic in soundproof, interference-proof booth), in the 1930s, the voices said, "This is G!" "Hot dog, Art!" and "Merry Christmas and Happy New Year to you all." Rather quotidian stuff for first electromagnetic contacts with the Great Beyond. But then, these were American ghosts. And listeners.

If the voices of famous living people could be heard in one's living-room, why not those of famous dead ones? Almost immediately after the disappearance of Amelia Earhart, after her last transmission to the USCGS *Itasca*, her voice was heard over the radio elsewhere. A teenage girl in St. Petersburg, Florida reported hearing Earhart's voice saying, "Here put your ear to it," and, "Are you so scared?"

*

Radio transmits disembodied voices, so it proved a perfect communication medium for the discarnate. Hesiod calls death "voice-robbing." But on the air—in the air—the voice is all there is. "Are there invisible entities adrift in the ether?" asks Jeffrey Sconce, adding, "Sound and image without material substance, the electronically mediated worlds of telecommunications often evoke the supernatural by creating virtual beings that appear to have no physical form."

The thought of spirits communicating via radio fascinated Nikola Tesla, even as he conducted early experiments with primitive crystal sets. "The sounds I am listening to every night at first appear to be human voices conversing back and forth in a language I cannot understand," Tesla would write in 1918, when there weren't many people broadcasting. "I find it difficult to imagine that I am actually hearing real voices from people not of this planet. There must be a more simple explanation that has so far eluded me."

Tesla felt these "voices" as Other—utterly outside his experience. He surely realized that a "more simple explanation" could be found in apophenia: in this case, the interpreting of a series of asemic sounds as language. Nonetheless, he would report, "My first observations positively terrified me as there was present in them something mysterious, not to say supernatural." And, he added, "I was alone in my laboratory at night." No one to witness and adjust, no one to drive the dark away.

Put your ear to it. See what it has to say.

*

In the 1960s and early 70s, Dr. Konstantin Raudive (1909-1974), a Latvian philosopher and translator, conducted research into what he called Electronic Voice Phenomenon (EVP). Under strictly controlled conditions, Raudive made recordings of what were apparently vocables emanating from the shortwave radio between assigned frequencies.

Raudive lists four uniform characteristics of these "voice-entities":

1. *The voice-entities speak very rapidly, in a mixture of languages, sometimes as many as five or six in one sentence* [fortunately, all of them European languages understood by the polyglot Raudive].
2. *They speak in a definite rhythm, which seems to be forced upon them by the means of communication they employ.*
3. *The rhythmic mode of speech imposes a shortened, telegram-style phrase or sentence.*
4. *Presumably arising from these restrictions, grammatical rules are frequently abandoned and neologisms abound.*

Needless to say, it took Raudive some time to learn to hear the entities; the same was true for others who participated in his "listening-in" sessions. Because "the voices are audible to our ear and we can understand that speech," Raudive drew the conclusion that they "must therefore be deemed to stem from a different plane of existence than our own." While that conclusion may not seem to follow from that premise, the researcher nonetheless "endeavored to understand the phenomenon in its factual sense"—though he notes (rather charmingly), "Faith and intuition can never harm a cause."

The voices seemed to know things that only certain deceased persons would know, so Raudive concluded that the "different plane of existence" from which they spoke was beyond the grave. He notes that "as the Latvian language is rarely heard on radio, one may safely regard messages spoken in Latvian as being of the same paranormal origin as those spoken in various languages." Raudive, a devout Roman Catholic, interpreted them as the self-expression of spirits—of souls.

He reports hearing "a voice tr[y] to form words out of torn vibrations that sound like the humming of a bumble-bee." He refers to such failed communications as "independent acoustic shapes," a phrase that suggests a more disturbing possibility— namely, that he was hearing voices independent of speakers, living *or* dead. Indeed, Raudive raises the possibility that the voice-entities "may use already existing human voice material."

In other words, what if the words were not being spoken? Perhaps our voices live on after us, freed from our will or consciousness, taking on a life of their own, whether they are recorded or not. But where did all the voices *go*, when the people were finished with them?

Even if language is not a virus from outer space, voiced words might replicate virally, apart from their former owners. Or perhaps the torn vibrations, the diluted residue of the utterances of a lifetime, recombine randomly, even as that life is still being lived.

The voices are frozen—that is where.

*

It's a short jump from believing in voices independent of human organs of speech and believing in the material existence of language apart from human volition. To the extent that language consists of marks on a surface or waves in the air, it exists independently of its origin, apart from will or intention, obdurately resisting authoritative interpretation; multivalent multiplying meanings, apart from individual expression, take on a life of their own. Thus voice, that most personal trait, the assurance of our unique individual identity, could be that which demonstrates our *lack* of uniqueness, our existence within a system of signs and other material objects.

Raudive simply presents transcriptions of utterances he has recorded in his researches, grouped by theme, with little interpretation added. As he says, "The voice-phenomenon must be allowed to speak to the reader directly." This procedure implies that the utterances are independent of intent insofar as the reader might interpret them quite differently from the researcher who recorded them or from the originator of the sounds.

This is a commonly accepted premise and practice among many poets of "the avant-garde tradition." Raudive calls on the avant-garde poet Mayakovsky; Mayakovsky replies (in Russian): "Konstantin, spit on it!" Raudive understands this gnomic utterance to mean "that I should not bother about what people say, but get on with what I think is right." Very well, Konstantin.

∗

Unlike Raudive's torn, buzzy voices, the ones I heard as a kid came through clearly, for many minutes, on the same frequency, speaking in a normal tone of voice at a normal rate. They said what they had to say many times, just to make sure the listener got it—whatever "it" was. Toneless random sets of five digits. Series of beeps like the tests of the Civil Defense alert signal. Vague rapid-fire Morse-code-sounding noises.

Voices climb on top of voices, trying to ex-press something, but disappear in aural haze. "Yahn-kee hotiel fox-troht," they say, over and over—hypnotized—along with interference from whatever is in the air with them (or it). "Group one zero text text." Then, "Message repeat repeat message message group one zero group one zero text text: [then many many numbers] . . . end of message end of message." Or a freaky tinkly music-box playing the "Swedish Rhapsody," followed by a child's impassive voice saying what sounded to me like German numbers, a different selection in a different order, each time—then the music box plays the tune over and over, then the same expressionless numbers, then the cheery rhapsody like an ice-cream truck—until the little one comes back on, then distorts into a more adult-sounding voice, over the warp of the waves. The music box winds down; the ballerina twirls more slowly. The child repeats sieben sieben sieben sieben eins sieben sieben sieben, until you wonder what the incantation could mean or do, then says "acht," which cracks like a cane. Then, "Ende." Dead air.

*

Even my dad didn't know what the voices were, and he knew a *lot*. But nobody knew what they were. I'd read about the Bermuda Triangle, about UFOs: these were the only logical explanations at the time. The disappeared or abducted planes and ships were trying to get out. Or the extraterrestrials were trying to get in. These null identities float above the suburbs   —   *Do they hear me listening?*   these bewildered last escaped signals   from officers sheared of their dimension   beckon me

this minute?   try to program us   , saying   *see ate-ate noon see diva*   souls stuck between known frequencies   begging us to listen   —*noon noon noon!* —
      tinny middeleuropean speakings   read your voice   in your head
crckl down the page
in our living
            room   or above   our house

jolly harmonium phrases   needle stuck

    (no getting off   this carousel)

*   *   *

Spies in the Living House

Author's Note:

The following poem is a "reading-through" of transcriptions of the utterances of "voice-entities" collected, via radio and magnetic tape, in *Breakthrough: An Amazing Experiment in Electronic Communication with the Dead* by Konstantin Raudive Ph.D. (Gerrards Cross, UK: Colin Smythe, 1971). Excerpts are sampled, rearranged, rewritten, misread, and combined with similar utterances; other phrases or lines are added by the present author. All of this is as the poem dictated.

Mother is here
Mother is with you
Let mother through

Mother is in the room
Mother hears
Mother speaks
Mother is on the tape

Mother is sick
Here mother cries
Over her lost child
cries your mother

Terrible forces array
against you – hold on!
Mother unites here

The moon is clear
Don't you see mother?
Mother is strong
We understand – step in

I cannot sing for you
Do not give in
in big things only

Mother, the first norm
Mother, farewell
we wait in the present

Leader, I am naked
My nerves could not stand –

I very small. You speak.
I know how to speak

There are many of us –
Cling firmly to this earth

Light the fire   the bridge
is here   The little one

is passive, dear, and radar
distorts the rhyme

Ready, even without
Truth, I am ready in the

Ninth house   Here is
gaiety – I will try to exist

Wild one you
pray on the lawn
That's right shoeless

I grew up Outside
I have been standing
very long time

Death is nothing
I am recuperating
This is how you

fix it – follow –
You are a little bit
involved –

You have the number
Speak through
At night we are always

fearful and nobody dares
There is yearning here
In the morning it is strict

The day is terrible
but taken away
Death is a real idea

I am always free she says meaning
I am here I am here give bread

The Professor of Non-Existence says
the body is the evidence of the head

Here are no longer few the thoughts
I leave cowering

The connection is steaming
Poor thing, he can't hear

Talk via radio? You
are the door

It is still autumn;
fashions are terribly vain.

Telephone with restraint,
Comrade. Here is here is

here it is the poor bridge;
Too long time is the sign.

Are you sleeping, poor
leader? One timely call –

There is no transmission –
you speak on command.

Radio on earth is scandalous;
it is a mess there

Terribly hot, terrible hurry –
we can see you going home

We are on the ship
We are spies in the living house
We are here in the room
We are the mad ones here

The night itself is sleeping
But I hope you can hear
this microphone voice
Do you? We hear *you*.

We can see you boy,
you are sleeping.
Those that think of us help us
Still too early, this deed

of the future   Transmit!
It is to your advantage
Your name is hidden
inside every line

Lord of hunger   Our father
mentions: hello, we are in flames
but there is no devil here

Believe us – we are the future
ones; here one bows the head
before the new existence.
The soul exists or you are hearing
the reverse of the soul, its impression
talking after the image is laid

Good schnapps   good coffee
souls in heaven   always thirst
Where are the guests?

You will serve as host, here
where cuckoos do not call
through silver birches
Though everywhere is spring
we miss twittering of birds.
O what the name of that flower?
Give us the voice and we know

all about change.
Fog smothers a lent light
there is no cream   the money
can be given to the shades

A multitude of voices:

Olga, who ironed your collars;
Pastor Diko, lilac again;
the exiled bishop;
We, Gerda, died just now, your Gerda
everywhere. Love Gerda!
And Irene whom you have lost.
Your Irene exists. Over here!
We are outside here.

Do you love me?
Do you hear us?
You knew me.
You remain.

I am alone. You are
without evening –
the bridge, please!
We are looking
all over the place for
human beings

You needed death,
you angel,
you are a bird.
Oedipus is dead,
incense is enough,
the soul calls a halt.
Leave it, my skeptic,
it is sufficient with the music.

We are standing in the corner with you.
We come beaten to you.

Where are you, dear?
Why are you attracting?
How can you hover in the cupboard?
We are going home through the radio.
Where do you want to go, son?

Spook

Dad would tune his smaller shortwave radio on the porch on fall evenings. Digital and solid-state, so not as precise or powerful. He smoked a Tiparillo as he found Radio Moscow, BBC, HCJB, VOA, and the other big-wattage stations—as well as a few smaller ones that couldn't be identified. The dog snooped around the yard and did his business and the crickets sang in dry October air.

When you live in a place like Memphis, you're helped by anything that might "expand your horizons." First, I arranged stamps from around the world in an album, each in its proper place, by continent and country. Later, shorwave frequencies and timetables. O the places you'll go—though they may distract you from what goes on in your own place or make you think anyone could go anyplace they please.

*

Even farther back, before the shortwave radio, on Wed., April 4, 1968, my mother and I were alone at our home in Memphis. My father was out of town, on business. I don't remember anything about that day. I was in kindergarten, I guess. I was about to start first grade in the fall. My parents would tune into the news report at 6 o'clock every night, and I probably tuned it out. On that night, though, something especially bad had happened far away, downtown, and it came into the home through the television set. I didn't understand it then and I don't understand it now. Papa was on the road and couldn't get through on the phone. Later, he would tell me that driving into Memphis during curfew/martial law was like entering a ghost town, meaning only ghosts allowed on the streets.

Still later, in fourth grade, I told a boy I was transferring to a Catholic school. He said I was going to a private school. I said no, it's a parochial school. A parochial school *is* a private school, he said, and I was leaving the public school because of busing. But I didn't think my parents would get mixed up in all that.

*

The dead might see the future as well as the past, but do they care about either? What the subject writes will be repeated, in as much detail as possible. It clings to the personal as long as it can—as "a polished representation of the life in question: a literary product whose narrative coherence as text stands for the assumed unity of the existence that is being described . . . ." In other words, a ghost.

The Father: This is a story about a snowman that didn't want to melt.

Child: Why didn't he?

The Father: Well, he didn't want to melt—he'd just turn into a puddle of water, and he wanted to stay a snowman.

∗

The way to communicate with the dead is to listen, to take note of *what they have to say*. Listening to audio tapes, for instance, or "listening" to photographs. The dead remain present as traces: the same remarks, the same expressions: repetition, not a new and living present.

And there you are, with them: looking at yourself just as they do. Your little cardigan sweater and shorts. Or in a child's voice, singing *"Good morning and hello! Good morning and hello!"* or talking about our extinct ancestors the dinosaurs.

How old were you, when you began to recognize yourself as represented?

Cicadas crawl from the earth after a human generation and molt, leaving a shell that is a perfect copy of what they used to look like. It clings, paperthin and delicate, to a treetrunk or post, with a slit down the back where the animate animal escaped. The shell is the flightless doppelganger, the fetch, of the winged insect. But the noisy adult doesn't even have a mouth.

I is an other, another other. Or it metamorphoses, gestates inside the shell of the self, given light by the phantom in the photograph.

I have no pictures of me at the radio (of even of the radio, which was sold for the vacuum tubes). We reinvent a memory every time it's used. Hence, we record them to keep them still. "Record" from *recordari*, lit. "to re-heart."

*

Who even *has* a shortwave radio anymore? You just go to the website and "Listen Now." Crystal-clear digital sound. Which is amazing for a former shortwave kid who built unclear crystal radio sets.

There's nothing spooky about listening to a podcast, even a podcast about spooks. Not like a photo or a piece of jewelry worn by the dead, hidden away in a case like an amulet, until you re-discover it. Such an artifact radiates absence. But digital sound? No sting, no punctum, no aura.

*

Meanwhile, the rich white dudes who rule the world yammer about transcendence via data, via digitizing subjectivity for later use, after death. Certainly, we are all surveilled enough to present ourselves from every angle, like Google maps. But can they really imagine a human being apart from a human body? Won't the purely virtual consciousness miss it, like a phantom limb? I suspect such a "consciousness" would always be aware of itself as immaterial, as lightweight, as simulacrum. Its very autonomy would point to the lack. The "mind" is itself because of the body; "to upload" is merely a metaphor without it. The me requires the not-me, who might be a Thou or might be You. One of them will have to ghost. *"Es spukt."*

The Silicon Valley futurists' future digital selves will still sound white, even without a body. *Because* without a body. But they can make themselves anything they want—can make *you* anything they want. They have the data.

*   *   *

Spies in the Living House

There are no slave-camps here
O yes there are slaves here!
You have seen death
bind death   obey death

We are not permitted to say
rules are eternal
We don't have any mail
That Lethe myth has clothed us

Here the world pleases but
we still miss the birches
In the city of the dead
there is no time
but many moments

We are naked, that is our law
We are liquidated
now we are human beings –
Here is a magic wand to bless –
One can hate so much!

Nonsense: learn to wade through
the heavy lack of music

You're below pitch, veering badly,
Channel 2! Your tape is vibrating –
Only through radio   Just let
the radio loose!   Better through
radio, through radio we accept:

Stay on one station – stick
with the spot – drive in the
middle, dance in the middle
do not come near the transmitter:

you yourself are radar
Contact with your world
esteemed a great deed
But contact *in* your world? . . .
It is narrow here

Compel you   postulated by you
We the departed are talking to *you*, Reader
We are in your debt, in your head and
we can't move on

Tune in correctly – terrible noises!
We are the expelled, lit by the red lamps

Lesson One: Hitler really lives
We talk of him a lot – his ominipotent friends

Remain calm – you had better speak German
We'll help you to hide in the garden

teamwork by the people of night
You know you will join us soon

This is operational   even the wolves
do not stay here   in the Uncertainty

Here the war never stops you know,
we never heard the ending

you knew it   the book

the world   does not believe

who of the lowest   are here

thank you   word

we are   for a name

love speaks   say something

the mask   surprises

in a hurry   go to bed

here are the tables   talk

I am a villain, do you understand? I have
beaten the weak   It is difficult for me here
I have not encountered death and yet
do believe this is the source   You
feel stupid in space   but you
are welcome here

Mister do you love the dead?
to die   it gives self-prize
It gives me wings
whoever you are   How much
do you believe in the living?

Where are you?
> *Our homeland free and sleeping*

What are you doing?
> *We want to meet you freely*

Why are you not here?
> *Vinegar without poison*

Why does the other not come?
> *You are chasing shadows*

Will one be visible here?
> *One can see you are waiting*

Who do you want mankind?
> *A voice with unhurried speech*

What do you want to say?
> *Disintegrating little earth*

Where are just scales?
> *The disappointment*

here sleeps time so
everyone fishes by night
by the pine torch light

the helpers
liked the bridge as it is
pleasant you understand
well you exist wake up

one is on the ship
a packet drawing nearer
you are the captain
Mother is deaf so
I longed to stay   to say

be glad exactly
the custom of the queen
here she is genuine clarity
but we are trembling
we are the language here

Mother is here –
don't you recognize her?
Call Mother   here is eternity

Wait! Mama   Mother
is working   Here
is Mother   here is me

Here is Mother   Mother!
Your mother Good morning
your mother

*   *   *

Spook

"Haunting belongs to the structure of every hegemony." (Derrida)

"These are what you suppose they are": it can be both confirmed and denied. That British official went on to add, "People shouldn't be mystified by them. They are not for, shall we say, public consumption."

It is virtually certain that the so-called "numbers stations" broadcast coded messages from spymasters to their operatives in the field. That is, the intelligence agencies used a global mass medium to communicate with a single listener or a small group. Although anyone could hear the messages, they went one way only; and the recipient could be anywhere, using any commercially-available shortwave receiver. By employing a "one-time pad" cryptographic system, in which the code changes from one message to the next, they were virtually unbreakable. This explanation accounts for the empirical evidence. Which is to say, the broadcasts I heard as a child indeed emanated from "spooks."

"Spook" was slang for "spy" by the 1960s, because the spy's job was to be invisible, to walk through walls, appear out of nowhere, appear as someone they weren't, vanish into a disembodied voice. Nobody knew what they did, which made what they did spooky.

This usage seems uncommon today. It arose in the heyday of Cold War, which makes it all seem so . . . so *analog*. It diminishes the numbers stations' mysterious, not to say supernatural, quality: "People shouldn't be mystified by them."

But radio still spooks, just as it did in 1918 (or the 1970s). You can be in total darkness and still you hear it. Lots of spooky signals still populate the spaces in between the stops, including a few voices repeating numbers. They speak from somewhere else, and you don't know how they look. But you know they are looking.

". . . ghost or *revenant*, sensuous-non-sensuous, visible-invisible, the specter first of all sees *us*. . . . We feel ourselves observed, sometimes under surveillance by it even before any apparition. Especially—and this is the event, for the specter is *of* the event—it sees us during a visit. It (re)pays us a *visit* [*Il nous rend visite*]."

*

But nowadays *everyone* recites lists of numbers, at least mentally. Credit cards, socials, phone, bank; dual-factor authentication for your accounts, using texted one-time codes; electoral votes; number of people in the room; word count; body count. 6 dead; 3 dead; 14 dead; 2 dead; 1 dead; 49 dead. Another day, another shooter, cop, count. It's turning us into ghosts, some sooner than others.

*

". . . administered forgettings and guarded secrets leave a kind of counter-evidence: material and spectral traces, shadowy aftereffects, and temporal disturbances." (Anne McClintock)

Just as there are radio-listening ghost hunters, there are numbers-stations aficionados amongst shortwave enthusiasts (or "DXers"). They record, triangulate, and report. They track the transmitters to military bases or embassies. They use empirical methods to solve mysteries. "The DX Files."

Conversely, EVP researchers use empirical methods to prove there is a mystery in the first place. For them, the important thing is not what the dead say, but that they can say anything at all: this is what they wish to prove.

*

By contrast, "Targeted Individuals" (TIs) have all the proof they need that spooks are real. The spooks are physical and malevolent. "Gang stalkers" harass them, bump into them, say things like, "Now you see how it works." TIs have to think the worst of everyone around them, because—well, who *are* those people, really?

Naturally, Targeted Individuals took to the internet to see if this was happening to anyone else, and, sure enough, it was—thousands of them. TIs began organizing to try to raise awareness of their victimization, support one another, and lobby for local resolutions against space-based mind-control. Their explanations offer a certain amount of comfort; as one psychiatrist put it, "You're not some meaningless nobody. You're being followed by the C.I.A." Unlike the DXers and EVPers, TIs try to *ignore* the voices. But how could you *not* listen? Maybe you really are being followed by the CIA. How would you know for sure that you weren't?

And how do you know the broadcast is not intended for your ears only? The media's "awesome powers of animated 'living' presence" gives it "a particularly sentient quality, figuring as a seemingly candid and intimate interlocutor engaged in direct contact with its (psychotic) audience (of one)" (Sconce). Like the spook, the radio is speaking directly to you. But unlike the spook, you didn't necessarily expect it. "Why me, Lord?"

*

But just because you're paranoid . . .

William S. Burroughs noted that EVP utterances have "a distinctive style reminiscent of schizophrenic speech . . . ." But he also suggested that perhaps "psychotic patients may be tuning in to a global . . . network of voices," even "a magnetic dome of prerecorded word and image" designed by the CIA.

Akin Fernandez, in his essay on numbers stations, "Paranoia Contamination," interprets the fact that the stations continued to broadcast after the fall of the Soviet Union as pointing to the greatest conspiracy of all—a conspiracy to continue the Cold War:

> When are the sabotage instructions to be sent, and what will the targets be? Will sleepers be awakened by a special codeword received whilst on a teabreak from waiting tables at the Dorchester? . . . And is the bus conductor on the No. 22 listening to the radio and writing down the results of the horses, or is he being told who his next murder victim is to be?

Whether these scenarios are realistic or not, there's no doubt that Russia, China, and the US still jockey for world hegemony and that spies are more active now than ever. You just don't see them. You don't see the nuclear missiles that still inhabit silos and tubes. You don't see the drone until it's too late.

*

Apophenia means perceiving patterns in random information (Why are all these people wearing *blue?*). But if you've found a pattern, is the information really random anymore? Look at the stars: you see a set of scales, I see a root; you see a goat with a fish's tail, I, an ox. You see a crab, I see a ghost. A semiotic Heisenberg Principle: "Reason looks for two, then arranges it from there," as poet Lyn Hejinian writes. Unreason does, too.

Indeed, since at least the 1910s, experimental writers have trafficked in apophenia, by forcing the reader to participate in the poem by supplying absent connections and context. Sometimes writers deliberately use chance procedures to produce random information; sometimes they find the patterns themselves by erasing all the words of a text except those that form the poem "hidden" within it.

Comparing the poet to the "madman" is a pretty tired trope by now. But poets, like schizophrenics (or Raudive's voices), make unlikely connections, make rapid transitions from one topic or thought to the next within the same sentence. Often, however, the poet (unlike the schizophrenic) has no clue as to the meaning of what they've just written down. There is no one-time pad, no decoder ring.

"Like ghosts, words are disembodied presences."

*

The poet Jack Spicer describes a moment in which William Butler Yeats' wife Georgie "began to have trances, and spooks came to her." But "these spooks were talking to *him*. . . . He asked, 'What are you here for?' And the spooks replied, 'We're here to give metaphors for your poetry.'"

Whatever the source from the Outside—whether spooks or Martians—for the poet (as for the adolescent shortwave enthusiast in the 70s), there's not much difference anyway. But writing down what's dictated from the Outside means setting aside one's personality, emotions, desires. "[C]an we take credit for our poems? Well, is a radio set a creator of the radio program?"

The poet as radio receiver: "you are something which is being transmitted into." Or, more accurately, you write down the signals transmitted, and you don't ask whence. To cinch the metaphor, Spicer refers to scenes in Jean Cocteau's film *Orphée*, in which the poet transcribes spooky sentences coming over a car radio.

*

Numbers stations began as early as World War I and were used in World War II as well. Radio Londres beamed Allied propaganda from the BBC's transmitters into Nazi-occupied France. The evening program, "The French Speak to the French," would often send out "personal messages" to individuals—thinly-disguised coded communiques to the Resistance. These took the form of often bizarre sentences. For instance:

> *Aesculapius does not like sheep.*

> *A cat has five extremities, four of them are sharp.*

> *Athalie stands in ecstasy.*
> *We repeat twice: Athalie stands in ecstasy.*

> *From Camille to Amicha: Six friends will find out that she bites tonight.*
> *We say: Six friends will find out that she bites tonight.*

The most famous of these messages was the broadcast of a stanza of Paul Verlaine's "Chanson d'Automne," containing the sentence: "The long sobs of autumn violins wound my heart with a monotonous languor." This passage meant that D-Day would happen in 24 hours.

In *Orphée*, we hear similar transmissions over that car radio:

> *Silence goes faster backwards. Three times. Silence goes faster backwards. Silence goes faster backwards. Three times. I repeat. Silence goes faster backwards . . .*

> *Attention! A single glass of water lights up the world. Three times. I repeat: A single glass of water lights up the world. A single glass of water lights up the world. Twice. I repeat . . .*

Cocteau later confirmed that the messages broadcast to the Resistance (which he and everyone else with a radio could hear) inspired the messages sent to his poet protagonist. Orphée becomes obsessed and listens to the radio non-stop while the car is parked in the garage. But rather than decoding these statements into more sensible instructions, he understands them as lines of poetry. "The least of these phrases is more than any of my poems," he declares. "They're on no other station. I'm certain they're meant for me." Like a numbers station, these are narrowcasts to one individual. Indeed, sometimes, only numbers come through:

> *38, 39, 40. Twice. I repeat. 38, 39, 40. 38, 39, 40. Attention. Listen: 38, 39, 40.*
> [rapid-fire Morse code. then:]
> *Attention. Listen: 2294. Twice. 2294. 2294.*

"What fascinating poetry!" Eurydice mocks, to which her husband quite sensibly responds: "Who's to say what's poetry and what's not?" He's just the one taking it down.

Many who have listened to the radio perceive it as transmitting the voices of the dead; but the radio station in the movie really does. Death (personified) and her undead helpers broadcast from their portable transmitter to the car radio. When they conclude the transmission, they pass through a mirror, which serves as a portal to the Underworld.

Death as a mysterious, dark-haired, hard-bitten princess; motorcycle riders in entomorphic military uniforms; a theatrical assassination and kidnapping; a ramshackle country seat as safe-house; tribunals and forced confessions; and a numbers station— all cloak-and-dagger, early Cold-War stuff. But instead of the CIA or KGB, these are Death and her undead underlings. Cocteau portrays the spooks as spooks. The "underworld" is the familiar haunt of both.

*

"Many operators documented rhythmic or robotic non-human sounding speech. Altered and shortened grammar and syntax" (Raudive, *Breakthrough*).

Numbers stations might well be transmissions from the dead: the person(s) who spoke the recorded numbers that are replayed in various combinations may in fact now be dead, as may the original founders and operators of the station. Some numbers stations seem to be automated, just as some voices are "artificial." Whether it's from behind the erstwhile Iron Curtain or from an undisclosed location, the discarnate sounds and voices keep repeating themselves, repeating the same numbers, regardless of their will. The messages are coming from the Outside—or the Other Side, perhaps.

And, as researcher Trevor Paglen notes, military research often spawns communications technologies: "New media, from the two-way radio to the Internet, often originate in research guided by a logic of seek and destroy, and hence they are always-already about human death," are about "military flight apparatuses, including fighter jets, surveillance planes, and satellites."

Spooks surveil. It's what they do.

*   *   *

Lincolnshire Poacher Variations

Author's Note:

This series began as an experiment in decryption (or maybe bibliomancy—fine distinction).

I began with a transcription of a particular 1990s broadcast from a particular numbers station. The station earned the sobriquet "The Lincolnshire Poacher" for using the first few bars of that British music-hall tune—repeated over and over and over—to begin its broadcasts (unsurprisingly, the station turned out to be British.)

There is meaning encoded within the numbers of the number stations. I want to get at meaning, when I can find it. But I do not have a one-time pad, a secret decoder ring to understand the voices. And the numbers may contain more meanings than one.

The numbers all have five digits. It has been surmised that the first three represent the page number in the pad, the second two, the line number on that page. The recipient would use the first word on that line, then repeat the process until a message emerged. This may or may not be the way the codes operate, but it is the method I adopted. At first, it occurred to me to use *Finnegan's Wake* as my one-time pad; it somehow seemed the natural choice. Unfortunately, my edition of the Wake clocks in at fewer than 999 pages. However, right next to it on the bookshelf was a 1970s edition of the *Norton Anthology of Poetry*. Very establishment and mostly English. Perfect for "The Lincolnshire Poacher."

Decrypting the transcription in this way produced the following raw result, rendered as a grid:

boy	was	for	sun	governors
with	leans	little	bones	bred
humors	is	with	it	thunder
when	dear	bore	white	how
loud	–	of	will	say
know	blossoming	night	and	who
thy	fall	the	gang	but
windows	did	splendor	no	and
town	hide	modest	accidental	will
the	and	and	know	the
Pluto's	time	kindly	bell	in
the	wilt	I	owene	the
wrought	Christ	plum	regent	and
instant	value	a	orchard	in
rest	tomb	the	through	yet
set	endless	widow's	of	did
am	although	me	came	there
alum	in	that	dew	name
with	be	trade	that	and
firm	like	thick	north	they

This raw result was less than satisfactory; it needed further decoding. Some phrases made some kind of sense: the Grid, like the "voice entities," was trying to communicate, but with stutters and incomplete utterances. So, I endeavored to discover what meanings might be haunting The Grid, by delving further into it, turning it, decrypting it using various generic keys.

time	tears	—	love's	Galien
a	a	he	quickness	to
but	they	mouth	fibrous	bigan
those	see	with	is	right
not	from	full	till	John
she	folk	through	from	ever
ripen	more	on	in	me
the	engraving	let	out	they
brim	done	the	to	sons
rocks	becalmed	the	blindfold	their
is	naught	and	sweet	are
druidic	saw	ought	praise	farewell
poppy	and	of	die	be
and	Ferrers	may	out	downright
tongue	celestial	worth	thence	gazer
leaves	of	beams	victor	sums
fair	with	on	our	the
thought	his	and	get	why
gazing	jet	in	will	darkly
reclin'd	am	this	while	mindful

[The Grid rendered in 14 lines, rather than the original 20:]

Sonnet

boy was for sun governors time tears – love's Galien with leans little while
bred a bones a he quickness to humours is with it thunder but they mouth
fibrous bigan when dear(e) bore white how tho(se) see with on with is right
of will say not from full till John know blossoming night and wilt who she
folk through from widow's of ever thy fall the gang but ripen more on in me
windows did splendor no and the engraving let out they town hide accidental
will brim done the to sons the and this and know the rocks becalmed the
blindfold their Pluto's time kindly bell in regent is nought and sweet are the
I owene the druidic saw ought praise farewell wrought Christ plum mindful
and of die be instant value a orchard in and Ferrers may out downright
rest tomb and the poppy through yet tongue celestial worth thence gazer set
did leaves of beams victor sums am although me cam(e) there fair modest
our the endless alum in that dew name thought his and get why with be
trade that and gazing jet in will darkly firm like thick north they reclin'd am

[an erasure of The Grid:]

Devotional (Garden of Gethsemane)

boy was for sun   time tears – love's

lean little bones bred   quickness

but they   began

white

–   not from

blossoming night

but ripen   on in me

the

modest   sons

know the rocks becalmed   blindfold

Pluto's   kindly bell   nought and sweet

ought praise farewell

Christ   regent and poppy

an orchard   may

rest tomb   yet   celestial   thence

endless   leaves of beams

came there

in that dew   thought   why

be trade   and gazing   darkly

like thick north they reclin'd

[The Grid with line breaks every 10 syllables, plus interpretive tweaks:]

Epic

Boy was for sun governor's time tears – love's
Galen with lean little bones bred an "a."
He quickens to humours, is with it thunder;
But they mouth fibrous, began when dear bore
White. "How those see with is right loud of will;
Say not from full till John know blossoming.
Night and whom she folks through every thy –
Fall the gang but ripen more on in me!
Windows did splendor not, and the engraved
Let out their town. Hide modest accident,
Will brim done thee to sons and know
The rocks becalmed, blindfold their Pluto.
Time's kindly bell is nought and sweet are
The wilt I own, the druidic saw ought
Praise farewell!" Wrought Christ plum, regent and pop,
And die be instant value, a orchard in
Ferrers may out down right rest tomb.
Through yet tongue celestial worth thence,
Gazer set endless windows did leaves
Of beams, victor sums. Am, although me came
There fair with our alum. In that
Dew, name thought his, and get why be trade –
That and gazing jet, in will darkly firm
Like thick north they reclined, this while mind.

[lines composed of word patterns isolated in columns of The Grid, read vertically, with interpretive tweaks:]

Song

know thy windows
the wrought instant
blossoming fall did hide

time wilt Christ value
bore of night the splendor
modest and kindly

sun bones white
came dew north
bred thunder

how say who
did there name
the brim rocks

tongue leaves
fair thought gazing
see from folk

naught saw in this
love's quickness
blindfold sweet praise

die out thence victor
downright gazer
sums the why darkly

[The Grid rotated 90° clockwise; lines composed of words selected from columns, read vertically, with interpretive tweaks:]

Meditatio

like thick north
am this while mindful
gazing jet will darkly
that dew name
although me came there fair

leaves of beams victor
celestial worth thence gazer
instant value a orchard
may out

christ-plum
regent poppy
Pluto's time   naught and sweet
know the rocks   the blindfold
their town hide modest
accidental will
done to the sons

windows did the engraving
let out thy fall
the gang know
blossoming night
folk through from ever
loud will say
bore white

how those see with thunder
they mouth little bones
for sun governors
time tears love's

[The Grid, rotated 180° clockwise; lines then composed of words selected from columns, read vertically, with interpretive tweaks:]

Pastorale

Mindful darkly, why the sums, gazer?
Be farewell.
Are their suns they? Me, ever?
John will get our victor thence.
Praise sweet blindfold! –
Love's worth may let on.
Full mouth, he reclined, gazing;
thought fair leaves ripen but a time.
They name who thunder bred.
North that dew came, through orchard;
bell knows no bones.
Sun, trade me widow's plum;
I, kindly and modest,
splendor the night with little.
Although endless, wilt time fall,
blossoming?
Dear is firm: set, rest.
The town's windows know.

[erasure of The Grid, rotated 270° clockwise, as originally revealed (roughly):]

Elegy

                                         sweet praise die   out
                                let the   beams   in
they see from folk more engraving done
                    ripen the   poppy   tongue leaves fair thought
              say who   will   name
bones   white   no   accidental bell
        with bore of night
           dear   blossoming fall   time wilt   value tomb endless
                  thy windows   rest   set   firm

[the preceding, relineated, left-aligned:]

Elegy

sweet praise die out

let the beams in

they see from folk

more engraving done

ripen the poppy

tongue leaves fair thought

say who will name bones white

no accidental bell

with bore of night

dear blossoming fall

time wilt value

tomb endless

thy windows rest

set firm

*　　*　　*

Re-naissance or *revenance*? . . . One does not know if the expectation prepares the coming of the figure-to-come or if it recalls the repetition of the same, of the same thing as ghost.

— Jacques Derrida, *Specters of Marx*

Dear Future,

Hope this message finds you well.
First off, let me say
it reassures me to know that
someone there is reading this, because
Future, you're my imaginary friend.
When we can't imagine
one another anymore, I'll be alone.

(dead vines fed upon by live juncos)

If I turned off the news, Future,
you would cease to exist.
So I make sure to record everything.
If you stay still, you might see the same things
that have always been there. Hence
Enlightenment is often couched in terms of an attack.

(The sound of dispersing consciousnesses.
A circle round the sun is called a glory.
Light is glory. It reflects the snow.)

I draw a circle around my feet and say
"This is my kingdom. The future is a theory
that doesn't involve me, a sleeve
that crumbles to dust when I touch it."
After all, I've lived longer than
most people who ever have.   But then,
writing has always been a suicide note.

Like they say: at the end of the day,
it's the end of the day.

And here we are: "Now"
is the bubble we're inside
that's always popping.

(Old salt turns
translucent crystal into dull white clots.
Hopeful green stuff; folding laundry. Flopping
like a stewed fish.   Who operates the squirrels?)

Future, you're like death: nobody knows what it is
until they get there, though plenty of people
claim to come back or even claim
to know what happened in the past.
I saw Jesus, back from the tomb,
standing amongst his disciples, saying
his last goodbyes (his *last* last goodbyes),
his robes brighter than the fuller's art,
apotheosing into the god of the sun,
levitating to his place amongst the constellations
to the tune of "It's a New Day Dawning!"

Future, I think you're composed of my thoughts
when they outrun my power to remember them.
Tomorrow, if I wake up, I'll say, "This is it –
the last day." Maybe then I'll remember.
Maybe then I won't have to write.
But every day seems like a day
more suited to going back
to the day before than
the day before was.

Future, you always run
away from us and we always keep chasing.
(I'd run from us, too, if I could.)
But dear Future, one can't live into nothing

indefinitely.   Exist!

(The wraith-like condensation:
heat vents in the morning –
like watching ocean waves or fish in an aquarium.
Ditto for the birds: they congregate,
spat, fly down to forage,
fly up to perch – Jacob's ladder or
fish with a bigger tank.)

What is holding you up, what
sounds from the other room,
how well I can breathe
compared to yesterday, since
the quality of light has changed.
Gravity refracts.   There are
specks and swaths of brightness,
but in the rest of the room, where
we live, the light is diffuse,
does not leave a memory to mark it.

We will be OK,
our palliative culture
the paregoric of heaven.
                        But there is
no We – just arrangements of I's:
Argus I'd.

What one person can do while un-
attached to outcome makes it a big short
drama or retrodiction of an insignificant flash.

                "The life of folly . . .
is entirely focused on the future," says Epicurus.
Which is pretty harsh.

Life as a period, life as a lull.
The new map of the cosmos
looks like an unpruned tree,
not a roadmap, so how can we
reinhabit the shape of the sky
before we outlive our endings?
What becomes of all the souls
when the sun finally explodes?

Really, we just want reliable apparitions.
Relatable apparitions.
I'm not there anymore, am I?

But the hour is late, and everybody
here looks pretty tired,
so I'll go ahead and say goodnight.
We will try not to wake you
when we get there.

Later,
J

*   *   *

. . . After blackness was invented
People began seeing ghosts.

— Terrance Hayes

Sp**k

Old Norse *spakr* "wise, experienced" and *spar* "prophetic" from IE *spek*, "observe" – whence Latin *specere*, "look" or *spectrum*, "image, appearance, shadow," so not invisible at all but *meant* to be seen – or not – short hop to

> *specter*
>> *spy*
>>> *spook* –

to be invisible while seeing or too visible while not seen to be feared
watching watchers watch out

spooked

*

"Spook" may have more to do with seeing than with hearing. Or not-seeing.

"Insisting on the black world's materiality is my starting point," writes Trevor Paglen. Indeed, his work revolves around uncovering and demystifying that "world of secret airplanes and unacknowledged spacecraft, 'black' military units and covert prisons, a secret geography that military and intelligence insiders call the 'black world.'" He is interested in "black sites" on the map—sites that, on the map, are actually not black but blank.

These places proliferated after 9/11 and are still going strong: "The black site prison program" consists of "off-the-books detention centers housing 'ghost' prisoners outside the Geneva Conventions and outside the purview of the Red cross . . ." Prisoners were/are not only housed, but also tortured (the notorious Abu Ghraib Prison was one such site). The Administration of George II (a.k.a. "W") gave the black sites its blessing. So, as Paglen puts it, "The black site policies, in effect, turned white. . . . Torture was now 'legal.'"

So, American spooks are part of the black world. Invisibility, but at will, unlike the ghost prisoners'. How do these spooks and ghosts appear? In the world of espionage and "intelligence gathering," black is white and vice versa, but everyone knows the chain of command and everyone knows to shut up.

"There is the question of cover,' said the general. 'An agent must be capable of fading into the background, adopting the guise of the person one cannot remember minutes after meeting him. Negroes in the field would be far too conspicuous.'" (Sam Greenlee)

*

"Ellison's Invisible Man gives double reference to both the unvisibility of the hypervisible African-American man and to the invisibility of 'the Man' who persistently needs an alibi for the blindness of his vision." (Avery Gordon)

"No, I am not a spook like those who haunted Edgar Allen Poe; nor am I one of those Hollywood-movie ectoplasms. I am a man of substance, of flesh and bone, fiber and liquids—and I might even be said to possess a mind."

When Ralph Ellison wrote these words, he did so with a full comprehension of the meanings that "spook" had acquired in the United States. In the opening sentences of *Invisible Man* (1952), the word means (literally) ghost. But it also means (implicitly) a mortal who has been categorized and rendered invisible—an extraordinary rendition. But this narrator is like a spy who has gone underground, but not (like a spy) entirely voluntarily; he is invisible because of his visibility, which determines what he is supposed to be when seen. Or rather, some see an appearance, an apparition, in place of the living mortal, to the point where "[y]ou wonder whether you aren't simply a phantom in other people's minds."

So, in his underground room, he sits thinking, ironically illuminated by the antidote of a thousand burning bulbs, in a hidden chamber of hyper-(in)visibility. "I can now see the darkness of lightness," he says. "I've illuminated the blackness of my invisibility—and vice versa."

*

Early descriptions and place-names [in the Hudson River Valley] suggest that the Dutch found Native Americans spooky; the Dutch in turn were cast as ghostly in the nineteenth and twentieth centuries. . . . Ghostliness in part served to articulate and contain anxieties about strange places and people. Wondering why a cave in Dutchess County was called the "Spook Hole," a newspaper reporter in 1870 was told that it had once been occupied "by an old man of foreign aspect [with] a negress and their son."

— Judith Richardson

*

"Spook" is a word that came into English from Dutch as a jocular way of saying that the speaker does not believe in ghosts—except as something quaint and rather superstitious—as a well-to-do Anglo New Yorker in 1819 might look back on the peasants of Dutch New Amsterdam as haunted by legends, rather than actual spirits of historical persons. In other words, it is a Gothic word. The Headless Horseman, after all, is not really headless, but no less creepy for all that.

"Sp**k" is kind of archaic, too, in the twenty-first century. Safely archaic, perhaps. Tim Roth as George Wallace in the movie *Selma* uses it; but even some younger African-American people do not know the usage or its history. So, even to discuss it may be like experimenting with the last smallpox strains at the WHO lab, when most people don't even know what smallpox was (or is). But if you're researching a word, you can't choose just the neutral meanings and avoid the spectral and dangerous ones, which will bump into you anyway. Now you see how it works.

There are those who don't believe in "sp**k" but know what it means. From a discussion of the word in the mid-2000s on *Urban Dictionary*: "A word to discribe [sic] a black person. Normally used by older [presumably white] folks in their mid 70's." Or: "Heard a 75-year-old Southern male relative use it 2 years back. I suspect it's going to die out altogether within my lifetime." To hear these young folks tell it, sp**k is no longer in use, except amongst a remnant community of hard-core racists in nursing homes. But other comments belie this premise. "Disparaging term for black people; used because during afternoon hours their darker skin tone blends with the darkness of the night, leaving only the whites of their eyes visible, thus resembling a ghost," writes "Tark Mwain." Ghosts as eyes only? "Valinda" is more specific: "a derogatory term to describe an intimidating black man who has invaded one's comfort zone."

"Comfort zone." The idea that one can only be comfortable inside a zone . . . like a Green Zone or safe zone. Which can be "invaded" but not really haunted. So, not a sacrifice zone or a Twilight Zone.

*

What, you may wonder, have I done to "sp**k"? Why have I replaced the o's with asterisks? I have punched its lights out. Because what are those o's but eyes? These eyes do not see you, but you may see them. In fact, you may have seen them already, staring from benighted minstrel shows, blackfaced actors in films, or caricatures (visual *or* verbal) in which the human visage becomes nothing but a spectral mouth and eyes.

A spook is a ghost or a spy, but sp**k means only one thing. Sure, the short form of the word "raccoon" has a non-racist usage, too; yet one seldom hears it in conversation (in public, anyway). Both words have a history; both are revenants. And each of them has those two circles staring out, to remind one of how they are seen.

"Moon,
        cantilever of sylabbles [sic]
 If it were spelled 'mune' it would not cause madness"   (Jack Spicer, "Morphemics")

*

Poets are people who hear and see patterns emerge—and rearrange them. So it would fall to another African-American poet and novelist to explore this connection of spook and sp**k. Sam Greenlee brilliantly invokes this confluence of meanings in his novel *The Spook Who Sat by the Door* (1969). The protagonist, Dan Freeman, becomes the first African-American CIA officer. After completing the agency's training program, he finds himself tokenized—sitting by the Company's door to advertise its supposed commitment to diversity. However, Freeman leaves the CIA and uses his experience to train a new rebel army of African-American freedom fighters who demand to be seen, heard and understood—by using machine guns and bombs. The book was made into a movie; in the DVD commentary, actor-director Bill Duke remarks, "I'm not exaggerating—I don't know how this film got made. . . . Tell me one person at Universal who'd approve this film being made today. Nobody."

Duke's remark is accurate, I suspect, because some obvious connections must remain invisible. In a scene in both the book and the movie, Freeman is playing pool with one of his former-gang-member lieutenants, who asks him if they can win their fight.

Freeman replies: "Who said anything about winning? We don't have to win; what we have to do is get down to the nitty-gritty and force whitey to choose between the two things he seems to dig more than anything else: fucking with us and playing Big Daddy to the world." White America can't play the home and away games at once: it would be too expensive to keep Black and brown folks down in the US *and* abroad at the same time, if both rebel at the same time (and those abroad were indeed doing so at the time). Freeman, having learned his lessons well at "the Company," wants to flip the script—turn sp**ks into spooks, reclaim power by spooking the white power structure. And for him, that means Pan-African militancy.

"We are organizing urban guerrillas in the United States according to the tactics inspired by Guevara, of creating two or three more Vietnams to bring the collapse of capitalism and imperialism," Stokely Carmichael had said, two years earlier—as recorded by eavesdropping US Army intelligence agents, who were some mighty spooked spooks.

*

It doesn't surprise me that literary America of c. 1820 embraced the old-fashioned "jocular" word for haints at around the same time that its pre-revolutionary days receded into a nostalgic bucolic past. Nor does it surprise me that the word came to mean both spies and a racial slur in the mid-twentieth-century United States. Both meanings have to do with making the invisible visible and the visible, invisible—a kind of topsy-turvy illogic of the deliberately Unknown. And both have to do with a particular configuration of power.

To hear the OED tell it, in the 1930s, "spooks" were originally house detectives. The "spook" was a "spotter"—"one who spies on employees" and "detects irregularities." This meaning is attested in 1942. Three years later, the *Hepcat Jive Talk Dictionary* would define "sp**k" as "a frightened Negro." For that moment, the same word could be applied both to the Black customer (or would-be customer) and to the employee shadowing the Black customer. Or, perhaps, the person shadowing the employee.

But the word would come to designate both the frightening agent from the Other Side (of the Iron Curtain or the mirror) and the "frightened Negro" at roughly the same moment—during the early Cold War, even as the postwar US Civil Rights movement and rising African nationalist movements were both being spied upon by the CIA, FBI, and European intelligence agencies.

"Spy vs. Spy" in *Mad* magazine, with its dueling black and white crows in trenchcoats and slouch hats: am I remembering this from childhood or imagining it as adult? Which is scarier? "Spook vs. Sp**k."

*

In 1964, 50% of white Americans sided with the "beloved" Hoover, 20% with King, as the former spied on the latter. "The reds" or "the blacks"—which scared white Americans more?

Back in the Memphis of my childhood, African-American people were indeed on the "Other Side," in more than one sense. The King assassination brought forth latent racial animosities and highlighted long-standing injustices that had festered for many years. But in white East Memphis, our geographical "comfort zone," it all happened "over there" somewhere. Like kids avoiding a "haunted" house, white Memphians didn't travel into "the wrong part of town." And nothing de-educates like segregation. We might as well have been on opposite sides of the Berlin Wall. I could find a Russian-speaking station in the shortwave bands; I could listen to WDIA on the AM end of the same dial. In both cases, the disembodied voices spoke from far far away. And we white kids in the early 1970s knew exactly what "sp**k" meant.

*

"To beat a body attempts to own it. And when the body cannot be owned, it must be extinguished" (mónica teresa ortiz). And murder is the ultimate form of objectification: to change a living being into an inanimate thing—pure body. How can that ever be worth it? For a bit more—what? Money? Power? Or maybe it's self-confirmation: there, I *did* that. Therefore I am.

White-sheeted night-riding ghosts are now "out," but not pasty-faced white boys in polo shirts, Fred Perrys, or camo, who say, in effect, "If we can turn you into an object, it proves we're real." Their own violent physicality as stereotyped uniform bodies makes them look all the more apparitional as individual volitional subjects—nothing more than sketchy poppits. But dangerous ones, because the Others have to play the ghost.

"You got to be a spirit. Don't need no more ghosts," adjures Amiri Baraka's character in the 1998 movie *Bulworth*. "I AM a MAN" = I am a living human = I am no ghost, maugre the powers that be. Even saying "I can't breathe" means you're not dead. Indeed, the chants of summer 2020 were manifestations of incarnate humans asserting physicality, their right to life and to matter, in more than one sense of the word. By comparison, the MAGAite seditionists of 2021—including their "storming" the Capitol—seemed to me dead souls herded by a necromancer, nattering like bats in a cave.

What scared them more? I think they were most scared of whiteness. Whiteness as ghostly. They looked in the mirror: there was nothing there.

Meanwhile, from the far reaches of the solar system, we all look like an imaginary dot. The human soul is a vestibule. The spirit is versatile, reversible, and can be a solid or whipt into a froth, spooned or poured forth from bowls.

*

"I'll see it when I believe it": I'm speaking *my* truth, *my* facts. I see the apparition, even if you don't. "Truth" from OE *treowth*, loyalty. Truth means plighting troth. Whatever you're loyal to is true, as far as you're concerned. Whoever you're loyal to speaks truth, regardless of resulting plights. We only believe the ones we believe we can believe. Once we do, we do: we take it in, take it down.

"Haunt" from *heimr*, home (Old Norse)—we haunt where we live, believing only in the other people there, never really leaving home or familiar haunts.

Knowing all this makes decrypting easy. You start to see the connections others cannot. Knowing the code means believing in your guts that you do. It's your "Spidey sense": you just *know*, you know? If 100s of people believe it, it's a conspiracy theory. If 100s of 1000s believe it, it's a conspiracy. 50 million Elvis fans can't be wrong: he lives. He's out there, sending signals back, warning you of enemies foreign and domestic, visible and invisible.

In other words, "you can tell just by looking." For the McMichaelses, that's all it took.

And always, other eyes watch: the drones & hidden cameras above—at stop lights, doorbells, store aisles, or in the bodiless insubstantiality of cyberspace. But also below, on phones.

*

Klansmen dressed up in white sheets to look like ghosts to spook the freedmen. The freedmen were the white folks' bogeys. The white-sheet "spooks" tried to spook those who spooked them—who were meant to be invisible. But the KKK were "terrorized by the ghost, the ghost of the other, and its own ghost as the ghost of the other" (Derrida).

George Zimmerman thought himself a Targeted Individual, not because of Trayvon Martin (who, it turns out, really was) but because of his own sight, scrying patterns out of thin air. Ferguson, Missouri police officer Darren Wilson said Michael Brown "had the most intense aggressive face. The only way I can describe it, it looks like a demon . . . ." Brown's "darker skin tone" blended with Wilson's image of what a demon looks like. And if "it" looks like a demon, well . . .

*

Why do people think of ghosts as being white? Because of diaphanous double-exposures? Maybe the old western dichotomy between the body—visible, heavy, sinful, earthy—and the soul—immaterial, light, capable of nobility, capable of floating away like a cloud.

But perhaps it's the other way around. Perhaps it's amorality, nihilism, narcissism, aimlessness, unreason, lack of raison d'etre; inhabiting your body while allowing the destruction of others'; being unwilling to see the apparition of all the faces in the crowd, as they appear—maybe it's these qualities that make one *less* substantial, less real, less serious. A dead soul does not make you sink into the underworld. It makes you dissolve while your heart still seems to beat. The voice is the last thing to go.

And maybe that's what we white folks are becoming, even while incarnate: disembodied voices yakking, ex-pressing our "selves," spouting opinions without solid values, bluster without character. What happens to other people's bodies does not concern us unless we can imagine it happening to ours, in which case we concern ourselves with ours. As lawyer and activist Abigail Dillen writes, "White people, and especially White men, perceive the risk least. For many people who have been comfortable until now, it is seemingly impossible to accept that anything so disruptive as climate change is possible." Or COVID-19. Or modern-day slavery. Those of us who are white males don't even think we *have* bodies: we don't have to. We fade in and out.

The opposite of black is not white. It is blank.

*

"Their personalities were fading. . . . As though, if you held the parents up to the light—if you could lift them easily, like paper—you'd be able to see right through them." (Lydia Millet, *A Children's Bible*).

What have white Americans *done*? We consumed. Excreted. Produced. Reproduced. Wasted. Consumed. Declaimed. But the past evaporated. The time is gone; we put the future in a safe place, and now we can't find it. I fear our souls are thinning fast.

Acknowledging death means you have to choose, in time. If you have agency, you choose consciously, according to some criteria, in the face of physical circumstances that may not conform to your will. You are a subject. If you put your foot down, you won't float away, even if you go underground. You carry some weight, in more ways than one. You are the thing of an hour who has made itself signify.

integrity = whole ≠ incorporeal

"serious," fr. Latin *serius* weighty, prob. akin to OE *swǣr* heavy, sad

But I suspect white folks believe we'll never die. And maybe that alone is enough to make us spectral, ghostly. We are living spooks.

*

And what about the poets? Are *they* targeted—with inside dope, orphic wisdom, malign intent, or anything at all? It's hard to hear Spicer's spooks dictating anything, nowadays. The Martians are departed.

But the dead, who are spirits of the past, keep coming back and hanging around: we are their natural home and host. Some poets and artists still hear them—but it's more likely to make you want to scream than sing. And who wants to read *that?*

Once upon a time, poets dreamed that poems would make them live forever. Their family and friends would toss their books into the sky, and the books would turn into birds and fly. The birdsongs would diminish until you needed a medium to hear them; one only has to discover who or what that is. And why we need to hear.

*   *   *

No escape alive or dead as long as Old Master rules, Fanon concluded many years later, writing about how some groups of people rule other groups of people by transforming those others into phantoms. The colonizer dooming invisible natives to ghost work. Scaring them with ghost stories of irresistible, godlike beke in charge during daylight hours, fearsome monsters and evil spirits reigning after night falls on the island. The circle unbroken.

— John Edgar Wideman, *Fanon*

The Eyes

it only took one look to know:

> "Is it his Mephistopheles beard? Or those
eyes,
> > rolling like billiard balls
> > behind his spectacle lenses? There is something
> > > terrifying about this man."

> Lumumba "picked the wrong side"
> proved too compelling
> > > *"specular experiences . . .*

HIS REMOVAL MUST BE AN URGENT AND
PRIME OBJECTIVE STOP THIS SHOULD BE
A HIGH PRIORITY OF OUR COVERT ACTION
STOP

> $100K hand-delivered to Agent Larry Devlin,
> > > > w/instructions:

poison Prime Minister's toothpaste –
"which would result in an illness
very similar to polio or something like that,
as I remember," adding:
> > "I'd never heard of the Agency
> > being involved in such a thing!"

> bad optics
> > > *extreme forms of human
> > > life, death-worlds . . .*

Lumumba made a run for it –
"Head him off at the river crossings. He has to cross
the rivers, so if you're there first,
well . . . you've got him"
                              – which they did,
            i.e. the Belgians,
            who delivered him unto the hands of
            Tshombe ("Cash Register"; "Le Juif") in Katanga,
            let him do the job, then dis-
            membered & dis-
            solved the bodies
            in battery acid

                    so mining companies
                    kept profiting off Katanga (then
                    & now: "click over to social media:
                      mother with baby strapped to her back
                      hacking at the earth under a scalding sun
                      trying to fill a sack
                      desperately, bent over, scrounging
                      cobalt for the smartphone in yr hand. Then
                      she can eat. Her baby can eat.")

                          vast populations subjected . . .

        or
    CIA tipping off
    S. African Buro vir Staatsveiligheid

                          to status of living dead (ghosts)."

                              *

"it is essential to see people . . .

Miss. "State Sovereignty Commission"
informants' "intel,"
deputies in KKK

        neutralize
        "charismatic leaders who are able
        to motivate people" –

                unseen & banished to the
                periphery of our social
                graciousness . . .

FBI's Wm. Sullivan, Aug. 1963, re: MLK:
    "We must mark him now
    as the most dangerous
    Negro in the future
    of this nation . . ."   which they did: Hoover

said: "racial situation is also being fully & continuously
        exploited by Communitsts
        on a national scale, so as to create
        unrest, dissention, and confusion" –

        quoted by Wallace –

                To mark one's place –

U2 over Birmingham –

Clarence Jones: "my wife said 'I didn't know
        you'd arranged
        for the phone company to work on our phones'"

because they can see you . . .

"King, I repeat you are done."
[*je le répète*: done, finished, done, done]

COINTELPRO   "running a
                             surveillance state"

          (still are – its flag that creepy
          white & black
             stars & stripes)

     newspaper carried his room #
     at the Lorraine
                         no police protection
          Memphis Chief
          from FBI year before

When the cops came, they ran
toward the Black people, not
toward the shooter, toward whom
the Black people pointed,

               who'd been on the lam for a year
          who spent 4 months
                    moving around Europe afterwards
                    w/ fake Canadian passport

Andrew Young: FBI behind it
                    they can address you."

          or
     Military Intelligence Division
          listening to Sunday sermons
          of King's grandfather (1917)

for evidence of subversion:

"It behooves us to find out all we can
about this colored preacher"

*

James Weldon Johnson stared
down at a pile of ash that had
recently been a man & thought
about "the sufferings of
the miserable victim" &
"the moral degradation of Memphis,"
about the "saving of black America's
body & white America's soul"

"Professional intelligence
analysts learn . . .

Bill Wilfong, the white girl's uncle
suspected "the negro, Persons,"
of the murder, remained undeterred
by lack of evidence –

"This is to certify that G. Hansen, the psychologist
[psychic] at 1120 Jackson Ave., Memphis, Tenn.
came to me, 5th of May, 1917, in search for
the murderer of Antoinette Rappel.
Mr. Hansen described
the scene of the crime, also a little
log cabin, where he said the guilty
one could be found, & also gave
a thorough description of
him & his wife
before he ever saw them"

you only had to see to know, even
w/ second sight

dangers of placing too much
faith in images . . .

or that of the dead:

take a photograph of the dead girl's eye,
advised the criminologist. The retina
retains the image of the killer there.

And sure enough: Officer Waggener
attested film showed Persons'
forehead & his hair,
a spectral image of
somebody's forehead & hair
in Waggener's retina

> *tends to support*
> *whatever truths observer*
> *is predisposed toward."*

"where [. . .] one could be found"

you only had to take one look to know

*

nowadays   cyber-Argus'   digital eyes –

                    Predator drones, Blackhawks,
                    electrical optical-infrared
                          Wescam MX-20 steerable camera turret
                    day or night, clear or haze:

                          DHS,
                          FBI,
                          DEA,
                          Natl. Guard, &

          surveilling
          Black Lives

          enhancing interrogation
          Black sites

"they changed the sounds
  to horrible ghost laughter . . .
  It got really spooky in this black hole"   (Khaled El-Masri)

                          CBP,
(an outside "whom"
 an inside "who"
 wants protecting from)

               (& pictures,   pictures

                              270 hrs. surveillance 15 cities

          into digital "Big Pipe,"
                          pumped to other police agencies

"The worst part for me is when we're made out
to be storm troopers," says the aerial spook

"gross abuse of authority," says the lawyer
"you see an aircraft, you have no idea
what technologies it carries"

"Stingrays" collect all cells'
call, text, browsing, location

                                        (listening   listening

        of "Black Identity Extremists" ⇒ they who
                "perceive racism & injustice
                in American society"
                (directed at them, that is)

                                        *"fuzzy, contradictory
                                        relationship* . . .

        "long-range, persistent video surveillance"
        aircraft registered to fictious companies . . .

facial "recognition" recognizes some faces

                grainy CTV photo picked out of lineup
                by guard who wasn't there &
                you're arrested for federal larceny

"I don't even live in Detroit and Detroit
 Police came to my house & carted me off" –
        30 hrs w/o food, water

"I've never been in trouble"

        but now you are, b/c

it only has to look to know
who it's looking for

between vision,
imaging, knowing, belief,
truth"

(what grainy image of the spirit
 will develop?

(what picture of what prophecy?

*   *   *

end of message end of message end of transmission

*   *   *

Sources

Aldhous, Pewter. "The FBI Used Its Most Advanced Spy Plane to Watch Black Lives Matter Protests." *BuzzFeed News* 20 June 2020. https://www.buzzfeednews.com/article/peteraldhous/fbi-surveillance-plane-black-lives-matter-dc.

Allison, Alexander W., et al., eds. *The Norton Anthology of Poetry, Revised.* New York: W.W. Norton & Company, Inc., 1975.

"Betty's Notebook." TIGHAR: The Earhart Project. https://tighar.org/Projects/Earhart/Archives/Documents/Notebook/notebook.html

Blanco, María del Pilar and Peeren, Esther, eds. *The Spectralities Reader: Ghosts and Haunting in Contemporary Cultural Theory.* London: Bloomsbury, 2013.

Brown, Kristen V. "Here's How the FBI Justified Spying on Black Lives Matter." *Splinter News* 8 Aug. 2016. https://splinternews.com/here-s-how-the-fbi-justified-spying-on-black-lives-matt-1793861001.

"Bullworth." Directed by Warren Beatty. Written by Warren Beatty and Jeremy Pikser. Produced by Warren Beatty and Pieter Jan Brugge. 20th Century Fox, 1998. DVD.

Burroughs, William S. "It Belongs to the Cucumbers." *The Adding Machine: Selected Essays.* New York: Grove Press, 2013 (orig. pub. 1985). 65-74.

Choudhury, Nusrat and Cyril, Malika. "The FBI Won't Hand Over Its Surveillance Records on 'Black Identity Extremists,' so We're Suing." American Civil Liberties Union blog. 21 March 2019. https://www.aclu.org/blog/racial-justice/race-and-criminal-justice/fbi-wont-hand-over-its-surveillance-records-black.

"Death Colonial Style : The Execution of Patrice Lumumba." Directed by Thomas Giefer. Produced by Solferino Images, Westdeutscher Rundfunk, and Quarter Latin Media. Film Ideas, 2010. Alexander Street, https://video.alexanderstreet.com/watch/death-colonial-style-the-execution-of-patrice-lumumba. See also Kucklick, Bruce, *Death in the Congo: Murdering Patrice Lumumba* (Cambridge MA: Harvard UP, 2015).

DeLeon, Radhamely. "Man Wrongfully Arrested By Facial Recognition Tells Congress

His Story." *Vice* 13 July 2021. https://www.vice.com/en/article/xgx5gd/man-wrongfully-arrested-by-facial-recognition-tells-congress-his-story.

Derrida, Jacques. *Specters of Marx: The State of the Debt, the Work of Mourning, & the New International.* Trans. Peggy Kamuf. New York: Routledge, 1994.

Dillen, Abigail. "Litigating in a Time of Crisis." *All We Can Save: Truth, Courage, and Solutions for the Climate Crisis.* Anaya Elizabeth Johnson and Katherine K. Wilkinson, eds. New York: One World, 2021. 51-59.

"Ell Persons: Research Materials." *The Lynching Sites Project of Memphis.* https://lynchingsitesmem.org/lynching/ell-persons.

Ellison, Ralph. *Invisible Man.* New York: Random House, 1952.

Fallon, Sean. "Build the Spirit Radio that Creeped Out Tesla Himself." *Gizmodo* 26 Oct. 2009. https://gizmodo.com/build-the-spirit-radio-that-creeped-out-tesla-himself-5390059.

Fernandez, Akin. "Paranoia Contamination: My Introduction to Numbers Stations." *The Conet Project: Recordings of Shortwave Numbers Stations.* Irdial-Disks/Notting Hill Music, 1997. 5-13.

Flores, Adolfo. "Officer Wilson: Michael Brown Looked Like A 'Demon' During Confrontation." *BuzzFeed News* 25 Nov. 2014. https://www.buzzfeednews.com/article/adolfoflores/officer-wilson-michael-brown-looked-like-a-demon-during-conf.

"Four more ways the CIA has meddled in Africa." BBC News, 17 May 2016. https://www.bbc.com/news/world-africa-36303327.

Gordon, Avery F. *Ghostly Matters: Haunting and the Sociological Imagination.* Minneapolis: U. of Minnesota U, 1997.

Greenlee, Sam. *The Spook Who Sat By the Door.* Detroit: Wayne State UP, 1990. Orig. pub. 1969, Richard Baron Books.

Hayes, Terrance. *American Sonnets for My Past and Future Assassin.* New York: Penguin Books, 2018.

Hejinian, Lyn. *My Life*. Los Angeles: Sun & Moon Press, 1987.

"Jean Cocteau 'Orphée' (1950)—Radio Transmissions." *Rorschach Audio*. 22 May 2013. https://rorschachaudio.com/2013/05/22/cocteau-orpheus-transmissions/.

Kanno-Youngs, Zolan. "U.S. Watched George Floyd Protests in 15 Cities Using Aerial Surveillance." *New York Times* (online) 19 June 2020. ProQuest Global Newsstream.

Kara, Siddharth. Interview. "The Ghost in Your Phone." *Throughline* podcast, 1 June 2023. https://www.npr.org/transcripts/1179117816.

Mbembe, Achille and Mitsch, R. H. "Life, Sovereignty, and Terror in the Fiction of Amos Tutuola." *Research in African Literatures* 34: 4 (2003). 1-26.

McClintock, Anne. "Imperial Ghosting and National Tragedy: Revenants from Hiroshima and Indian Country in the War on Terror." *PMLA* 129.4 (2014) 819-829.

McPhate, Mike. "United States of Paranoia: They See Gangs of Stalkers." *New York Times* (online) 10 June 2016. ProQuest Global Newsstream.

Millet, Lydia. *A Children's Bible*. New York: W.W. Norton & Company, 2020.

"MLK/FBI." Directed by Sam Pollard. Produced by Benjamin Hedin and Tradecraft Films LLC. Film Platform, 2020. Alexander Street, https://video.alexanderstreet.com/watch/mlk-fbi. See also Garrow, David J., *The FBI and Martin Luther King, Jr.: From "Solo" to Memphis* (New York: W.W. Norton, 1981).

"Numbers Stations." *DXing.com*. Universal Radio Research. https://www.dxing.com/numbers.htm.

O'Gorman, Marcel. *Necromedia*. Posthumanities 33. Minneapolis: U of Minnesota P, 2015.

"Orphée." Andre Paulve Film. Réalisé par Jean Cocteau. Films du Palais Royal, 1950. Criterion Collection, 2000. DVD.

ortiz, mónica teresa. *autobiography of a semiromantic anarchist*. Austin, TX: Host Publications, 2019.

Paglen, Trevor. *Blank Spots on the Map: The Dark Geography of the Pentagon's Secret World.* New York: Dutton, 2009.

Paglen, Trevor. *Invisible: Covert Operations and Classified Landscapes.* New York: Aperture, 2010.

Peters, John Durham. *Speaking Into the Air: A History of the Idea of Communication.* Chicago: Univ. of Chicago Press, 1999.

Rankine, Claudia. *Citizen: An American Lyric.* Minneapolis, MN: Graywolf Press, 2014.

Raudive, Konstantin. *Breakthrough: An Amazing Experiment in Electronic Communication with the Dead.* Trans. Nadia Fowler. Garrards Cross, UK: Smythe, 1971.

Reichert, Corinne. "House Dems Demand FBI, Others Stop Spying on Black Lives Matter Protests." *CNET Tech* 9 June 2020. https://www.cnet.com/tech/services-and-software/house-dems-ask-fbi-others-to-stop-spying-on-black-lives-matter-protesters/.

Richardson, Judith. "A History of Unrest." Blanco, María del Pilar and Peeren, Esther, eds. *The Spectralities Reader: Ghosts and Haunting in Contemporary Cultural Theory.* London: Bloomsbury, 2013. 489-506.

Roach, Mary. *Spook: Science Tackles the Afterlife.* New York: W.W. Norton and Co., 2005.

Sconce, Jeffrey. *Haunted Media: Electronic Presence from Telegraphy to Television.* Durham NC: Duke UP, 2000.

Sebald, W.G. *Austerlitz.* Trans. Anthea Bell. New York: Random House, 2001.

Segal, David. "The Shortwave and the Calling." *Washington Post* 3 Aug. 2004: C1.

"Selma." Directed by Ava DuVernay. Written by Paul Webb. Paramount Pictures, 2015. DVD.

Spicer, Jack. "Vancouver Lecture 1: Dictation and 'A Textbook of Poetry.'" *The House that Jack Built: The Collected Lectures of Jack Spicer*, Peter Gizzi, ed. Middletown, CT: Wesleyan Univ. Press, 1998. 1-48.

"Spies of Mississippi." Directed by Dawn Porter. Produced by Dawn Porter and Trilogy Films. Public Broadcasting Service, 2014. Alexander Street, See also Bowers,

Rick, *Spies of Mississippi: The True Story of the Spy Network that Tried to Destroy the Civil Rights Movement* (Washington, DC: National Geographic Books, 2010).

"Spook." *Oxford English Dictionary.*

"Spook." *Urban Dictionary.*
https://www.urbandictionary.com/define.php?term=spooks&page=2.

"The Spook Who Sat by the Door." A Bokari Ltd. Production. Screenplay by Sam Greenlee, Mel Clay. Produced by Ivan Dixon, Sam Greenlee. Directed by Ivan Dixon. Monarch Home Video: Obsidian Home Entertainment, 2004 (orig. prod. 1973). DVD.

Tompkins, Stephen G. "In 1917, Spy Target Was Black America." *Commercial Appeal* [Memphis] 21 March 1993: A7+.

*   *   *

Joseph Harrington is the author of *Of Some Sky* (BlazeVOX Books); *Goodnight Whoever's Listening* (Essay Press); *Things Come On (an amneoir)* (Wesleyan); and the critical work *Poetry and the Public* (Wesleyan), among other works.